MW00613411

BATCHERY: VOLUME THREE

© 2021 Marcus V. Calvert

By Tales Unlimited, LLC.

For permissions, contact: https://www.talesunlimited.net.

Cover by Lincoln Adams

Edited by Alexandra Hupertz

ACKNOWLEDGMENTS

I'd like to thank Lincoln Adams (my cover artist) for his time, patience, and wicked-awesome skill.

Rose, thanks for keeping me in the game.

To my editor and beta readers, thanks for your irritating eye(s) for detail.

To everyone else who had a hand in this twisted thing being written (living or not), I thank you.

I must also tip a hat to my fellow artists and strangers-turned fans. You truly are a hip crowd.

Here's how it works:

1.   Flip past the "Intro" section, to any random page. Pick a writing prompt that catches your eye. **These prompts aren't etched in stone**, so feel free to tweak them as you see fit. So, if you hate vampires, turn the vampire prompt into something else.

2.   From that prompt, create a short story with a beginning, middle, and end. **DO NOT** try to turn it into a novel (yet). Try to keep it under 3,000 words (unless the story goes there). The purpose here is to help you develop a stable writing routine, finish what you start, and discover your storytelling preferences.

3.   Try to complete the story in 5-7 days (or sooner, if you can). Go to another prompt and turn it into your next story. Then repeat this process 98+ more times.

4.   When you've written 100 or more stories, copyright them as one bulk property (Google the "**Library of Congress-Copyright Office**").

5.   Now do you write that novel? Nope. Pick 20-25 short stories and turn them into your first book. Try to find something they all have in common. My first anthology series ("Unheroic") was about unlikely heroes saving the day. Try to find a title that **ISN'T** on the Amazon website. Something unique, clever, and easy to pitch to an audience.

6.   Download some (free) Grammarly software. Use it on your work and find the typos. Google articles about "**fiction self-editing rules**" and "**grammar rules in fiction.**" Surf the articles and compile a checklist. Will this replace your need for an editor? No. Still, you can erase some bad habits from your technique early on.

7.   Polish and re-polish your short stories until they're all as good as you can make them. Then polish them three more times. If you have to swap out a story or completely rework it, go ahead.

8.   Once done, you'll need two or three beta readers. I'd recommend hard-core movie geeks or anyone who can sniff out plot holes in anything they see. Offer payment and insist on a thorough read-through with sincere feedback. Do believe that good betas will find stuff that you missed.

9.   Start shopping around for editors—preferably someone who understands what you're trying to do. I'd recommend using a PayPal account (for easy payments and easier tracking, at tax time). To find that editor, start with word-of-mouth referrals from anyone you might know in the writing game. Also, you could plug "**fiction editor searches for beginners**" into Google. However you find that editor, ALWAYS pay by the word (not by the hour).

10.   Hit Google and type in "**free text to speech download**." Pick something that works well in Word and let i read your book to you. It's slow and plodding . . . but utterly worth the time. After the betas and editor are done with it, give your book one last listen—just in case some error slippec through the cracks.

11.   Where do you get your books published? That's up to you. If you're going through a traditional publisher, I'd start with Google and talk to writers who've gone through the process. From what I've seen, getting a publisher is a time-consuming nightmare. Personally, I'd rather self-publish (for now) because my books are mine and I can control how they're dropped. If a legit publisher tracks me down, then we'll talk.

Now, if you self-publish, do your homework.

As of this printing, I'd recommend Amazon KDP. Three reasons spring to mind.

One, readers like to buy their books/e-books from Amazon—for reliability, quality printing, and quick delivery. They only charge you (wholesale) for the books you buy, not for being on their website.

Two, publishers and self-publishers are dropping like flies in this competitive market. Amazon (for now) is the most stable way to self-publish.

Three, self-publishers have to charge more—both for their services and their books. They'll likely put your books on Amazon anyway, which only costs you more of your royalties. If you're worried about ownerships, copyright each of your books and buy ISBNs in bulk (Google **"Why should I buy ISBNs?"**).

12.   Whether you self-publish or not, consider banging out a few anthologies (with 20-25 short stories each). Folks still like to read short stories and will buy yours (if you hustle it right). Appealing cover art's a solid idea as well. Find an "eye candy" moment, in one of your stories, and make that your front cover. Sometimes, a great cover sells the book for you.

Why not start with that novel yet? Simple. The short stories are done and edited—just waiting to be sold. So sell 'em. I began with 180 short stories, self-published three anthologies, started an LLC., and hit every live-selling event I could find (from conventions to open mics to craft shows). I didn't bother with online marketing because the field's too crowded. Instead, I ordered a supply of books and signed up for vendor slots. Find the large crowds and/or go where the geeks gather. Both tend to be sympathetic to a passionate up-and-comer.

Find gigs, buy vendor spaces, and learn how to sell to people. If you want to wait until your second or third anthology is done, that's fine. You'll have more time to save up a war chest. My point is that an author with three books should sell better than an author with only one. Hustle your polished works with confidence and hone your chops. Then your fan base will gradually form and demand that novel.

13.   **NOW YOU WRITE THAT NOVEL**. With all of those short stories you've knocked down, a book concept should emerge. Also, you can pluck choice ideas from past works (from plotlines to odd characters to useful concepts).

If you can plot a book, good for you. Hit Google for a plotting method that suits you.

If you can't outline to save your life—like me—it'll be harder . . . but better. Why? Because you have no idea how your book will end. You'll knock around draft after draft until the book's as good as you can make it. The struggle is its own reward. Still, it wouldn't hurt to look through Google, under "**Novel Writing for Pantsers**." Maybe you'll find something of use.

However you write your novel, expect to write drafts you'll set aside. Save them anyway. Flawed drafts might have choice bits that can be salvaged later on. Label and save them in a file somewhere (just in case). Then finish the damn thing. Don't rush it. Rewrite whole chapters (or even the whole thing) if you must. When it's done, run it through the polish/beta/edit process, copyright it, and slap a cover on that puppy.

14.   Keep writing short stories (both to cook up new ideas and to stay sharp). Also, you'll need material for future anthologies, right? Imagine you're at a comic con table with two anthology series to your left and a novel series to your right. Toss in a "2 for $20" discount for flavor and make your pitch. True bookworms (or people shopping for them) will be sorely tempted to buy from you.

Many authors diss short stories. Ignore them because short stories sell very well in "live" settings. That's because anthologies have more possible pitches than a novel. Also, short stories are a faster proof of talent than a 70,000-word novel.

15.   If you decide to self-publish for the long-haul, write a will. Do estate planning and find an executor. If you don't have some kind of succession plan, your literary legacy might die with you—and that would be a shame.

16.   One Last **Purely Optional Step:** Pass this on to struggling writers. That friend or relative with more imagination than confidence. These prompts could help them.

Good Luck!

BATCH #41

401 – One night, you walk past an outdoor neighborhood cour and stumble across a spectral match (complete with ghost audience). What's the sport?

402 – Rather than directly invade the Earth, a mischievous alien race decides to quietly use one nation to take over the world—but which one?

403 – Your brilliant daughter becomes a freelance terrorist with a flair for explosives. Her crimes are so horrific that you come out of retirement to hunt her down.

404 – After claiming a nine-figure lottery prize, you decide to spend it (for the greater good) as an "undercover elitist."

405 – A homeless man has become insanely hungry for meat and nothing else. Things get to the point where he's willing to eat anything (or anyone) to make the incessant craving go away.

406 – A day in the life of the Devil's personal assistant.

407 – Frankenstein's monster becomes a rather brilliant Victorian-era detective.

408 – You derive your potent super power(s) from mouthwash.

409 – A renowned martial artist gets kidnapped and sent centuries into the future (or past, if you prefer). Why?

410 – Death hires you to rescue his therapist.

BATCH #42

411 – A lucky spy infiltrates a high-end arms bazaar for mad geniuses.

412 – Just before Halloween, you buy a *very real* wizard's hat at an estate sale.

413 – During a hostage rescue, a new super hero team loses it leader. One of the hostages, a hard-core gaming geek, steps up and starts barking brilliant orders.

414 – An evil corporation enslaves one alternate Earth after the other—until they find yours.

415 – What would it take for a modern-day serial killer to become a respected folk hero? To the point where even some cops look the other way?

416 – You're a human bouncer at a bar for demons . . . and your job is never easy.

417 – Two daffy hijackers decide to rob a five-star restaurant, simply because [insert stupid reason].

418 – You can see through the eyes of anyone who has been murdered within a mile of you. Instead of seeking justice, you seek opportunities—because you're evil.

419 – A highly advanced alien race comes along to evict the entire human population from the Earth—wait. What?!

420 – A team of angels arrives in a remote desert to swap souls with a team of demons.

BATCH #43

421 – Patient zero of a pending zombie apocalypse is begging you to put down the gun . . .

422 – On a fantasy world, a talented thief must steal a vampiric blade from a truly gifted (and crazed) swordsman.

423 – How would a deity go about getting his/her stolen powers back?

424 – You go on a blind date. By the end of it, you're stranded in a fantasy world.

425 – A futuristic film studio sends a capture team into the Old West to "recruit" some authentic characters for its next film project.

426 – For some odd reason, everyone doubts your honest statements but believes *any* lie you tell.

427 – Never, ever break a woman's heart—especially when she's a shapeshifting dragon.

428 – When in danger, the descendants of a fallen samurai clan might end up possessed by one of their legendary ancestors.

429 – A leprechaun gets into the collections business for a loan shark.

430 – The sister of a bloodthirsty cartel boss asks for your head. Why?

BATCH #44

431 – A pack of geniuses and psychics start their own spy agency—while still in grade school.

432 – You overhear your parents arguing about whether or not to kill you now . . . or wait to see if the "monster emerges."

433 – You're a street reporter who specializes in gossip tales regarding both super heroes and villains. Tonight, you're pursuing the story of the year.

434 – You anxiously man a trench as a Nazi "D-Day" invasion force hits your position . . . some ten miles from Washington D.C.

435 – Alien spies plan to grab a black ops legend, who's returned to Earth for a family reunion.

436 – A superhuman black ops team is escorting an escaped politician across a war zone, toward American custody. Your job' to kill them all.

437 – You have to kill both of your kids . . . or countless lives will be lost.

438 – A team of government agents chases a dangerous, shapeshifting alien into a massive cosplay convention.

439 – Someone mailed you magic sandals for Christmas.

440 – Why (oh why) would you steal millions from your angerous boss, then recklessly gamble it away?

BATCH #45

441 – Someone just bought up the marker on your soul.

442 – There's a new bioweapon out there. Inject it into a fresh corpse and it will rise as a feral killing machine.

443 – During the daylight hours, people ignore your presence: no matter what you do.

444 – You're the poor schmuck tasked with test-driving a prototype spy car.

445 – In the middle of a police raid, the surviving bad guys turn into werecreatures.

446 – In a bar, two people argue over which killing methods (in movies) are realistic and which aren't. One is a grizzled movie geek. The other is a semi-retired assassin.

447 – A super hero interviews for a slot on the hippest new crimefighting team.

448 – Some poor fool just bought a used vanity mirror, with emonic glyphs etched around its frame.

449 – A vampire is leaving sex tapes at multiple crime scenes. Vhether he/she shows up on film is entirely up to you.

450 – A secret agent is confronted by a class-action lawsuit— or child support—by the many, many women he's knocked up ver an illustrious career.

BATCH #46

451 – A vampire stands trial for allegedly feeding on others o
her kind (for the blood high).

452 – The human girlfriend of an alien spy gleefully tells him
that she is pregnant, just after he recommends a full-scale
(genocidal) invasion of Earth.

453 – Someone's cursed you in such a way that you're actuall
grateful.

454 – A ruthless psychic has stolen a world-class talent from
your mind. How can you get it back?

455 – Out of love, a time traveler risks reality itself to meet
her favorite author and "nudge" him away from a tragic destiny.

456 – Three nights per month, your uncle's ghost can freely
walk the mortal coil. Needless to say, the old ghost is quite the
scoundrel.

457 – During your lengthy prison sentence, you protected the
weaker inmates with your fighting skills. Now that you're almost
out, your closest friends are at risk. How can you protect them
(without picking up more time)?

458 – A dealer sells you and your buddies some bad drugs. One of you dies. The rest of you recover and plot some messed-up revenge.

459 – Your newborn twins both grow up within eighteen hours, complete with an education and knowledge of pop culture. What are their intentions?

460 – You're a super hero with a family. One day, via text, someone threatens to reveal your secret identity—unless you complete an unscrupulous suicide mission.

BATCH #47

461 – Amidst the crossfire of a futuristic gang shootout, paramedics try to save a dying SWAT cyborg.

462 – What if the Age of Super Heroes began in the Old West? [Free advice? Think past just steampunk.]

463 – You've just been executed by lethal injection. As your soul leaves your body, the warden gets a frantic call to stop the procedure. Apparently, you were found innocent after all. Pissed as hell, you decide to . . .

464 – While flying a fully-armed fighter/warbot, your system get hacked. You try to regain control as your plane shifts into warbot mode and starts to level a major city.

465 – Someone is sending letters laced with an alchemical mind control ink. Anyone who reads these notes is forced to commit crimes in your city.

466 – You're a retired tomb raider who has been approached with one last, irresistible job.

467 – You're stuck on a public toilet in a Mexican standoff with a masked gunman? Now what?

468 – You wake up handcuffed to the steering wheel of a speeding car with no brakes.

469 – A kid bribes his tooth fairy to get even with a bully who's also about to lose a tooth.

470 – A serial killer is chasing a quartet of big game hunters through a remote locale.

BATCH #48

471 – A time traveler is about to get her head lopped off in an unpleasant past. Why?

472 – You laughingly bear witness to a running fistfight between two well-trained mall Santas.

473 – A suicidal convict gets a hysterically wise comedian as a cellmate.

474 – In a fantasy world, you've just saved the fair princess and helped her ascend the throne. Then she orders you put to death?!

475 – A lethal, airborne zombie virus is unleashed upon a massive cruise ship. Within a short span of time, thousands of hungry undead hunt the few (immune) survivors.

476 – It's trash day and you're walking past a row of garbage bins. You hear a whimpering sound from one of them . . . and the sound is almost human.

477 – You mug an old lady, who grins as you shove her into a darkened alley at gunpoint.

478 – Overnight, someone broke into your little tattoo parlor. They ignored the money and made off with your special piercings: the ones which can augment a spellcaster's magic.

479 – In a dystopian future, the Olympics have become quite deadly.

480 – A boring corporate employee happens to be the last scion of an ancient, mystical bloodline—one that competing dark forces have a vested interest in.

BATCH #49

481 – You get arrested for saving the Earth.

482 – Scotland Yard hires you to recover Excalibur.

483 – You wake up in a buried coffin and struggle to remember how you got there.

484 – You must persuade a disgruntled geneticist not to unleash an incurable pathogen upon a major city.

485 –Your late aunt leaves you the deed to her automated gadget factory.

486 – A hitchhiker passes a rustic field, just as massive creatures start to hatch from bundles of hay.

487 – Death offers you a job.

488 – Three days after you kill a cop, he (or she) comes gunning for you—rotting flesh and all.

489 – Someone has summoned a pack of mythical creatures to kill you.

490 – You've been assigned to investigate the disappearance of a super heroine.

BATCH #50

491 – An ex-con must decide whether/not to snitch out a terro plot.

492 – Your very fast car just skidded sideways off a very high cliff. The car is a mangled pile of flaming debris but you only have a few bruises?

493 – You fall asleep in your bed (alone) and wake up next to a beautiful corpse—with her blood all over you.

494 – What if the descendants of Robin Hood formed a secre clan of monster hunters?

495 – Researchers capture a vampire and starve her out, hoping to understand the process. What goes so very wrong?

496 – A pair of grizzled nerds take a shy "virgin man" out to nightclub and give him some seriously clever tips on picking up women.

497 – What would the U.S. be like if the Democrats (just to make a point) only competed in local and county elections, while forcing the GOP to govern the country?

498 – It's the 1970s, on a dark street. A white cop, a tough-
ooking black guy, and a cute white chick pass each other on a full
oon night. One is a hungry werewolf, one is a monster hunter,
ıd one is a racist (your call). What happens next?

499 – A renowned hero of the realm gets banished to the Earth
.ane because of his love for the king's daughter. A decade later,
ıe daughter (now someone else's queen) comes groveling to him
ır help.

500 – You arrange a black market art auction worth millions.
 lot of influential (and dangerous) people send reps to bid and
ɔu stand to make a tidy "finder's fee." You arrive a bit late to find
 lot of bodies, spent shell casings, and no art.

BATCH #51

501 – You're chased through a mall by the knife-wielding father of a girl you bullied into killing herself.

502 – You're trying to wrangle a date with the hot gal next to you . . . in a passenger jet that's falling from the sky.

503 – A dozen giant, rampaging monsters are on their way toward a city of millions. How can you stop them, without resorting to nukes?

504 – Movie geek aliens kidnap an Oscar-winning actress and declare her their High Empress.

505 – A serial killer's digital trophy gallery just got locked up by some hacker's ransomware. What happens next?

506 – A dying gunslinger passes on his enchanted Colt Peacemaker to a brave young lawman.

507– You've unknowingly moved into a remote, family-friendly town with a population that is about ninety percent extraterrestrial.

508 – A failed songwriter turns to the occult to salvage his
ıreer—but won't sell his soul to do it.

509 – Some crazed geneticist went and made your dog a
lekinetic!

510 – A mad scientist is about to retire and wants to sell his
ıiminal empire.

BATCH #52

511 – Space mercenaries land on a Separatist colony, with orders to restore order: by any means necessary.

512 – A pack of young super villains goes on a campaign to prank super heroes and film it all.

513 – You win way too much money on a trip to a casino. Management has pulled you aside, ready to accuse you of cheating. Little do they know that getting "caught" is only part of your real scheme (whatever it is).

514 – You break into a small art gallery to steal a rare painting, only to have it try to kill you.

515 – Your evil twin needs a life-saving, triple-organ transplant and plans to harvest yours—even though it'll mean your death.

516 – In a dystopian future, select children are genetically augmented and trained to defend the state from any and all threats—without mercy.

517 – You've been tasked with investigating the cause of a nuclear incident in your hometown.

518 – A day in the life of a blinded ex-villain.

519 – You walk past a tatted-up guy. When his tats glow at our approach, he freaks out and pulls a knife on you. Why?

520 – The ghost of a murdered thug haunts your neighborhood. Some say he's good. Others call him evil. What's his story?

BATCH #53

521 – You're eating in a restaurant. Then you notice a guy's reflection walk along the restaurant's mirrored interior. It kills a young woman's reflection. Seconds later, the woman herself just falls over dead. That's when the killer's reflection makes eye contact with you . . .

522 – At some point in the 22nd century, the Cleveland Browns finally win their first Super Bowl. You've been assigned to report on the celebratory downtown rioting.

523 – A tired crimefighter returns to his mansion's basement lair, only to catch his girlfriend in the process of sabotaging his gear.

524 – An eccentric relative leaves you a solid gold toilet in his will, with strict instructions not to melt it down. You do it anyway (and make a fortune off the gold bricks). What are the consequences?

525 – A long-neglected lair decides to find a new hero (or villain?) to replace its prior tenant.

526 – There's this guy who always does the right thing . . . and pays for it every time. Make it comically sad, where he seems cursed to always fail.

527 – Your SWAT team's evacuating citizens from a massive
superhuman street fight. One of the heroes gets knocked out with
lesser minions looking for an easy kill. Do you intervene?

528 – Christmas carolers break into your home. They're
actually singing as they try to kill everyone inside.

529 – Aliens discover a post-Apocalyptic Earth and send
advanced AIs to pose as gods. Why?

530 – An old lady collects stray cats and turns them into
talking familiars (for her Wiccan clients).

BATCH #54

531 – You're falsely convicted for murder and sentenced to d
hard time. Even worse, someone's pulling strings to get you killed

532 – A spy, in her third trimester, goes into labor during a
wild car chase/shootout.

533 – A drug dealer finds himself looking into the murder of
his favorite client.

534 – You're late for a zombie run . . . only to realize that
these zombies are all too real.

535 – A group of grizzled bikers gets 'jacked and killed by
rural cops, while delivering millions in drug money. Too bad the
cops left one of the bikers alive . . .

536 – There's this antique guillotine that was used in the
French Revolution. It's supposed to be haunted by a ghost with a
thing for beheading rich people. And a wealthy bidder's just
brought it home from auction.

537 – A therapist tries to inspire combat vets with PTSD to
put their pain into story form.

538 – You're asleep (upstairs) when two men crash through
our living room window, apparently locked in a vicious fight to
e death.

539 – In times of intense stress, a little girl's deadly imaginary
iend can possess her—and do whatever needs to be done.

540 – You're a journalist who's investigating five seemingly
irelated murders. Why do you care? Well, each victim was a
impire buddy of yours.

BATCH #55

541 – The biggest geek in high school steps onto a talent show stage with a couple of other geeks . . . and cuts loose with a Grammy-level performance.

542 – You're being chased downhill by well-armed, sexy, murderous women on skis. Why are they shooting at you?

543 – A corporate-designed assassination AI is being field-tested on you.

544 – You awaken from a drunken bender with a folded-up contract (for your soul) in your lap. What did you sell it for?

545 – What if you were a defense lawyer who specialized in super villain crime cases?

546 – Archaeologists find an ancient tomb, open it up, and (to their horror) find . . .

547 – Santa Claus learns that his bank accounts have all been hacked by someone naughty.

548 – Cops crash a packed wedding and start making arrests. Why?

549 – An alchemist mass-produces a popular hot sauce, which ꞁes what to the taster?

550 – You're trapped in a burning building (facing certain ꞁath), when time suddenly stops around you—but you're not ꞁfected. Now what?

BATCH #56

551 – You stumble out of a parent-teacher conference with a concussion and two black eyes. Why?

552 – You own a thick mystical diary, which allows you to jump into any (past) day that you've chronicled.

553 – Sixteen dangerous people are dropped off on a remote island and forced to play a deadly game. The rules are twisted and there can be only one winner.

554 – During an earthquake, a frightened child's telekinetic abilities surface.

555 – Your soul gets kidnapped in front of a group of mystics who drop their coffees and rush to your aid.

556 – You volunteer at a homeless shelter for supernatural creatures who are down on their luck.

557 – An angel and a demon quietly vie for your soul.

558 – A hostage negotiator must deal with a pack of spectral kidnappers with a serious grudge.

559 – A group of former sidekicks meet at their heroic mentor's grave . . . only to find it empty.

560 – A pair of pagan gods run into each other in an Old West town.

BATCH #57

561 – An unemployed cancer patient goes on a crime spree to pay the medical bills.

562 – A crew of bank robbers rushes out of a bank, just as someone carjacks the getaway vehicle.

563 – The good news is that you escaped from Hell. The bad news is that your escape didn't go unnoticed.

564 – A retired super hero has taken over as the warden of a prison for the world's most dangerous super villains. Describe a typical day.

565 – You're a foreign medic doing humanitarian work in the U.S., during its second Civil War.

566 – Scientists realize that dogs are immune to the zombie virus and try to figure out how best to use them.

567 – What if a mystical spy could make a target's art "snitch" on the owner(s)?

568 – Your anti-Christmas rap is so controversial that someone pays you a murderous visit on Christmas Eve.

569 – A rigidly routine crook hops out of the shower and gets
essed while fending off a team of assassins.

570 – A planetoid (full of aliens) parks itself near the Earth's
oon. Your space fleet's been tasked with making first contact.

BATCH #58

571 – You're a tabloid reporter whose latest story's not only false—but likely to get you killed.

572 – In a crime-ridden future, each cop serves and protects under the watchful "eyes" of an AI judge and jury.

573 – A planeload of modern-day British soldiers gets caught up in a weird storm and crash-lands on American soil . . . during the Revolutionary War.

574 – Aliens invite humanity into an interstellar collective, with access to much-needed technology and vast economic opportunities. There's just one condition . . .

575 – A psycho killer's conscience implant has malfunctioned. He/she now walks the streets, looking to make up for lost crime.

576 – An up-and-coming street gang messes with the wrong sidekick's kid sister.

577 – You've been brought in to investigate the mysterious disappearance of two members of the British royal family.

578 – Massive alien spheres approach the planet and shrink 4% of the population within a matter of seconds. Can the maining 6% save the day?

579 – A wealthy time traveler goes back into the past to botage the success of his famous ancestor, who'll create a onstrous corporate dynasty.

580 – You come home just in time to spot a thin black tail sappear down your wife's throat.

BATCHERY #59

581 – A traumatized vet always has the backing of her troops—even the dead ones.

582 – A mob boss gets his memories tainted by a vengeful telepath.

583 – A retiree is driving along, witnesses an intentional hit-'n-run, then ends up chasing the killer through the streets of a major city.

584 – Someone (or something) unleashes a devastating plague upon your realm. Innocent victims stay dead. Those trained in violence come back . . .

585 – A chatty mall guard spots a potential mass shooter and tries to talk him down.

586 – Your silly little nightmares aren't just becoming true, they're becoming worse . . .

587 – Every time one of your relatives dies, your bank account mysteriously goes up by a lot of money. Why?

588 – As you're about to commit suicide, a demon comes along and politely asks if you'd like to trade your soul for a second chance.

589 – Your breakout music video has been banned in fourteen countries (including the U.S.). Yet, it's also the most passed-around clip on the Internet. Why?

590 – Four lawmen look after your post-Apocalyptic county. They're quite crazy-cool, especially when a massive outlaw gang comes to town.

BATCHERY #60

591 – An author with writer's block goes on a crime spree to come up with ideas for his next book.

592 – A team of techno-ninja creeps into a training camp for super spies, with orders to kill them all.

593 – Other people's tattoos talk to you—and only you can hear them. One particular client's tattoos are begging you to stop him from killing another child.

594 – A masked crew of bank robbers gets pulled over (for a routine traffic stop) while on the way to a heist.

595 – The Speaker of the House learns that the President and Vice President are both missing.

596 – Write out an episode of a reality show about super villain housewives.

597 – Over drinks, three accomplished super spies swap tales about their closest brushes with death.

598 – You buy a used car, only to find a ghost in the trunk.

599 – During a World War III aerial dogfight, alien fighters warm in and start laying into both sides.

600 – You're in the middle of a high-speed car chase . . . rough a major wildfire.

ABOUT THE AUTHOR

Marcus V. Calvert is a native of Detroit who grew up with an addiction to sci-fi that just wouldn't go away. His goal is to tell unique, twisted stories that people will be reading long after he's gone.

His books are available on Amazon.com and Kindle. You can also follow him on:

*Facebook:
https://www.facebook.com/TalesUnlimited

*Website:
talesunlimited.net

*Twitter:
https://twitter.com/MarcusVCalvert

*YouTube:
https://www.youtube.com/playlist?list=PLjxE-sCVpsVem5yD5J-dPjHGDYbyYaIIi

*TikTok:
Tales Unlimited Marcus V. Calvert

CURRENT TITLES

Short Story Anthologies

The Unheroic Series

Unheroic, Book 1
Unheroic, Book 2

The Book Of Schemes Series

The Book Of Schemes, Book 1
The Book Of Schemes, Book 2
The Book Of Schemes, Book 3

Novels

The I, Villain Series

I, Villain
Murder Sauce
Frag Code
Coin Game

Writing Guides

The Batchery Series

Batchery, Volume I
Batchery, Volume II
Batchery, Volume III

Made in the USA
Middletown, DE
21 June 2022

67397255R00029